An EAGER CHILD

Growing up in Norway

The childhood story of Vida Engh
born: Ovidie Hagen
Elverum, Norway
1889

Betty F. Engh Pettersen

Illustrated by Elva Hurst

WestBow
PRESS
A DIVISION OF THOMAS NELSON

ISBN: 978-1-4497-4296-6 (sc)
ISBN: 978-1-4497-4297-3 (e)

Library of Congress Control Number: 2012904656

WestBow Press books may be ordered through booksellers or by contacting:

WestBow Press
A Division of Thomas Nelson
1663 Liberty Drive
Bloomington, IN 47403
www.westbowpress.com
1-(866) 928-1240

Printed in the United States of America

WestBow Press rev. date: 5/02/2012

An Eager Child

Growing up in Norway

Only known child photograph of Ovidie

Eager
Defined

FEELING OR SHOWING KEEN DESIRE; IMPATIENT OR ANXIOUS TO DO
OR GET; ARDENT; SHARP; KEEN;- - - - IMPLIES DEEP INTEREST
AND A SPIRITED READINESS TO ACHIEVE SOMETHING

PREFACE

June 1989

From the original Memoir, <u>Ovidie,</u> written for the
Celebration of
Mother's 100th birthday

We have set forth a simple childhood story of our mother's growing up in Norway. She was a country girl, and her nurturing place was on a small isolated farm where for generations her family had maintained what can only be described as a 'self-sufficient, self-contained lifestyle'.

Mother shared precious little about her childhood. She was faith based, a private person by nature and stayed generally attentive to the present-breakfast, lunch and dinner, the mail, news and weather, sewing, knitting, mending, and keeping her life structured and in good order. She was not given to nostagia, reviewing past hurts and joys, or to sentimentality. She was not prone to look back- - - - -until she was nearing her 100th birthday celebration.

Three pictures emerged from safekeeping and she was elated! The pictures were from her childhood in Norway-the family's farmhouse, the school she had attended and the Lutheran Church where she was confirmed. When they were framed and hung for her to see through the day, we stared in disbelief as she pointed them out to everyone who visited. Family and friends were interested. Questions about her past began to emerge. As more old pictures and facts surfaced in preparation for her life-celebration we reflected with gratitude on her journey from ambitious little farm girl in far-away Norway to the intrepid Mother with whom we had experienced life together all of these decades. It was time, we decided, to put together a Memoir, a tribute of thankfulness, if you will, to include family information and focusing on our mother's growing up in Norway were in our opinion the roots of her life-patterning had been well established, and had in fact, impacted our own up-bringing in the most positive of ways.

So we started with the three pictures mentioned above, and reflected back on the threads of events which our mother had felt worthy of mention in the past. This childhood storybook is our attempt to have the beloved Farm and Farmhouse, the Schoolhouse and the most cherished Elverum Kirke, the Church of her up-bringing 'come alive' by infusing these precious childhood scenes with the significant people, activities and the bits of her shared memories from the past.

From the 'precious little' shared have come the glimpses, now fondly recalled and recorded as perhaps they most likely could have happened. In truth, there really were: bows from Christiania, summers and picking berries at the 'hytte,' shoemaker's shoes, dressmakers coming to the home, never-to-be-forgotten Christmas Eve traditions with family, gjetost snacks at the neighbors, stories of a young boy who came to live with the family, sewing on Sunday, milking Mama's cow, Mama's midwifery in borrowed trousers, Papa's carpentry and coffin boxes, brother Aksel's school teacher friend and above all, her Lutheran confirmation.

The family facts are accurately detailed.

Putting these family facts and recollections on paper brought new delight, for Mother with whom its progress was shared, and for our family, too, the delight of new understanding, perspectives and relationships with appreciation for our hearty, highly motivated and caring forebearers.

As we get to know Ovidie, the strong-willed, industrious and courageous little Norwegian girl in her story, we also come to know and admire the proud lady about whom the story is written. Our mother, Vida Engh, has indeed moved steadfastly forward in her life-journey with the kind of determination and courage rooted and nurtured in her childhood.

It is with great joy that we celebrate our intrepid Mother's gift of longevity, and with gratitude celebrate her legacy of life-lessons for all of us woven ever so quietly, but intricately into the fabric of her well-lived life.

Daughter, Betty,
For sisters, Ruth and Dorothy, too
June 1989

FORWARD

Celebrating Life

We knew to expect a host of people to be with us for the Open House in celebration of our mother's 100th birthday. They came- family from afar, friends from everywhere, church folk, co-workers, neighbors, even members from the Sons of Norway Lodge, some with accordions to sing and play throughout the afternoon; and what's a gala event without reporters with cameras showing up! Here was a celebration of our past and present unfolding like a pageant before us!

We were overcome with gratitude to God and guests for this response and for the blessings of our life-journey represented by each person's presence.

The original version of Memoir <u>Ovidie, The Childhood Story of Vida Engh, Born Ovidie Hagen, Elverum, Norway, June 14, 1889</u> printed in booklet form and presented to all who came, was well received. Many found places indoors and outdoors to peruse, read and respond to the little book that provided a story line of our mother's courageous goal-directed journey to this point of celebration.

OVIDIE

**The Childhood Story
of
VIDA ENGH**

*Born Ovidie Hagen, Elverum, Norway
June 14, 1889*

Mother lived in the glow of her Life Celebration,

periodically reviewing her Memoir,

for another year,

until passing to her heavenly home

exactly on her 101st birthday

June 14, 1990

. . . . .

Vida Engh about whom this book is written lived simply, but with purpose.

Her childhood story of growing up in Norway is, therefore, intentionally set forth as she lived 'simply, but with purpose'.

Recording the facts of a family's past is not only fascinating, it is fraught with opportunity for being amazed about the how of what unfolded in the lives of those before us has, in truth, not only brought us to where we are now, but may still represent an ever-present generic influence. So, for reflection comes this storybook written with a passionate "Takk for alt!" and as a tribute to a strongly rooted and well-grounded Norwegian immigrant mother.

Betty F. Engh Pettersen, Daughter
Spring 2012

CONTENTS

COUNTRY HOUSE

In your imagination draw a HOUSE--

a simple country HOUSE.

Make it square,

with a slanted roof,

a door in front,

a chimney on top.

The HOUSE is made of lumber.

The lumber is weathered.

Think of the HOUSE you are drawing

as sturdy,

in good repair,

and very old.

Ovidie's birthplace and childhood home - a small farm in
Elverum, Norway on the banks of the Glomma River.

Set the house down on a flat space of ground in the mountains.

Ring the house with large clumps of old evergreen trees.

Allow just enough clearing around the house for a number of smaller buildings for the animals.

Oh yes, the house should be on the bank of a wide, smooth and fast flowing river that is also wooded on both sides.

The river is good for fishing.

Draw in a wide path from the house on through the trees and down to the edge of the river. The people who live in the house you are drawing will want to go down the path to the river to fish.

The picture of the house and the setting is now complete.

It is the setting for the story of a special young girl.

The story begins- - - - - -

Ovidie's Brothers and Sister

Marianne

Aksel and wife, Signe

Peder and wife, Dordi

Family

The house is on a farm. The farm is named HAGENLAND.

HAGENLAND is the home of AKSEL AND HANNA HAGEN, good hard-working parents who are older now. Their children are 'almost grown':

PEDER, the oldest, works with his father who is a carpenter and cabinet maker. They take orders and work at Hagenland. Peder is soon to be married and will leave the farm to make a home for himself and his wife.

AKSEL, named for his father, is smart and strong. He is an apprentice in the village metal shop. When he has learned the trade, he will go to Christiania*, the capital city, to find work and live there.

MARIANNE is lame and is not quick to learn. She is good-natured, is taught at home, and helps with all of the household chores.

Aksel and Hanna Hagen are proud parents. It is their belief that if children grow up healthy and work hard, they will do fine in life.

Peder, Aksel and Marianne have learned not only to work hard,
    but also to work steadily,
        to work carefully,
            to live frugally and to save money.
They go to church on Sunday,
    read from their Bibles,
        say their prayers.
            They have been confirmed
            in the Lutheran Church.

Ja, alt skal bli bra med barna!
Yes, all will be fine with the children!

*The name of the capital city, Christiania, was changed to Oslo in 1925.

Family And Farm Names

BJØLSETHAGEN
HAGEN
HAGENLAND

The FAMILY NAME for centuries past was
BJØLSETHAGEN
(Be-yelt-set-hog-an).
It was
shortened in the 1800's to
HAGEN,
not an umcommon practice in that era.

The family continued to use
BJØLSETHAGEN
for legal matters as noted on
Ovidie's Christening certificate and on
Papa Hagen and Mama Hagen's
grave markers in
Elverum Kirke Churchyard.

The FAMILY FARM, likewise, continued to be referred to
as BJØLSETHAGEN, and in fact is to this day.

But, for this childhood storybook the
FARM name, BJØLSETHAGEN,
has been Anglicized to
HAGENLAND
(Hog-an-lond)
for easier reading and pronunciation.

HAGEN, IN NORWEGIAN IS 'THE GARDEN'.
HAGENLAND, THEN, IS THE 'GARDEN LAND' OR 'GARDEN PLACE'.

Yes, HAGENLAND in this storybook is the name of the simple
farm in the most
beautiful of settings in Norway, and indeed, is the
GARDEN PLACE IN WHICH OVIDIE'S
GROWING UP WAS NURTURED.

We go back one hundred years to the house in the setting we have just pictured.

The house is already many decades old when the story opens.

There are lights in the windows.

Smoke is rising from the chimney.

This is a busy house,
     a warm house,
          a caring home,
               a home where everyone has a role. . .
               and a goal.

Clouds pass over the home,
     and the sun comes up.

The Farm late 1800's

Ovidie's Christening Certificate

Dåpsattest.

Kirkeboka for   Elverum   sokn i   Elverum   xx by/prestegjeld

viser at   Ovidie

søn/datter av foreldre Selveier Aksel Pedersen Bjølsethhagen

og hstr. Hanna Mathiasdtr.

er født den   14/6- 89- fjortende juni a. h. ni og otti

i   Elverum

og døpt den   8/9- 89 - ottende september s. å.

i   Elverum

Elverum sokneprest- embete den 10/6- 49   19

sokneprest

Lovbestemt betaling kr. 1,00 — en — krone.

Dǿpefatet

Osgå kirkens døpefat er eldre enn kirke-bygget, og er hentet fra den gamle kirken.

Det er laget i messing, og viser Adam og slangen i Paradis, altså en sydefallseberetning. Døpefatet har følgende inskripsjon: <<Maren salig Knut Andersons har Foraeret dette til Elveroms Kieche Aar 1672.>>

Christening Urn, Elverum Kirke, Norway

But, as this story begins, Aksel and Hanna as parents, also carry a heavy sadness.

    They have just lost a lovely and gentle, ever-so-frail little seven year old daughter

    named Ovidie.

Despite the efforts of caring parents,

    despite the protectiveness of the brothers,

       and the loving attentiveness of her sister,

         young Ovidie passes slowly and quietly away.

Everyone feels the loss.

 # New Baby Girl

But, the story moves along.
It is a year later-June 14, 1889.
A new baby girl is born to Aksel and Hanna.
The birth is a surprise!
An unexpected happening! But. . .
it brings joy.
It lightens the sadness
of a grieving family.
It seems as though the new baby is sent to be
the little girl that they have lost; and so,
she is given the same name.
The new little baby girl is christened
Ovidie in the summer of the same year.

Unlike her gentle and frail sisters,
Ovidie is healthy and active,
a good learner,
clever and skillful,
strong willed.

Ovidie is the last child born to Aksel and
Hanna Hagen.
She is the center of everyone's attention. . . . .
a star revolving in her own universe!

Learning To Bake

"Kom her!" Ovidie is excited. Mama
has given her a bit of bread dough to make into a
small loaf.

> The wooden table is too high for a three year old.
> She stands on the bench and is calling everyone
> to "come here" to see the lump of dough crudely
> shaped, resting on the table.
>
>> "Peder", she calls.
>> "Aksel, Aksel, Aksel", the toddler
>> yells. Aksel comes. He is always
>> attentive to the baby.
>> Marianne is already with Ovidie. She
>> seldom leaves the baby's side.

Mama looks up just in time to see laughing little
Ovidie, having gained everyone's attention, pick up
the dough and in her excitement toss it toward
the wooden beamed ceiling. She screams with glee.

> But, oh! The dough sticks on the wooden beam.
> Everyone laughs.

"Now it's gone," says Peder, "too bad".
Ovidie is not laughing now. She looks
appealingly to Aksel.

> "Gone, all gone says Aksel. "Your bread
> would have tasted good. "
> The baby does not stop.
>> "My bread, my bread, my bread", she cries.
>> She is frustrated looking from one to the other.
>> She whines a bit and then stamps her foot.

"Peder, get the baby's dough," Mama says.

> He does.

Ovidie is happy again, settles down and
carefully remakes her tiny loaf of bread.
Mama is pleased.

The baby is learning to make bread

"Ja alt skal bli bra med barna."

The goat gets extra hugs

SKIS FOR OVIDIE

Papa favors Ovidie.
She is active.
She is playful.
She is fun.
She has just turned four!

Papa is watching Ovidie play with the goat. Papa is sitting on the bench he just made. He made two benches one for the front of the house and one for the back. Papa had the wood 'on hand'. "Be good for you and me to rest a bit" he said to Mama. She just looked at him. "No resting" she thought. She knew, like Papa knew, that the benches were made so that someone could sit and keep track of little Ovidie.

"She is all over the place" thinks Papa, and then says to Mama "Our boys, Aksel and Peder, played by the house. Give them a puddle and some bits of wood----no need to worry about the boys. But, this little one" and then he shared his thoughts, "She's all over the place, wanders off. Takes someone to watch her--give her attention!" "Ja", Mama agrees as she turns and goes into the house.

Ovidie and the goat are special pals.
Ovidie feeds the goat,
strokes her,
rides her, and is
learning to help Mama milk her.

Papa lights his pipe. He squints to get a better look at Ovidie. He is looking at her strong little legs as she climbs on and off of the goat. As he puffs his pipe he decides "Yes, she is ready! Ovidie is ready to have me make her a pair of skis. Winter will be coming. She should have skis!"

Anxious now to tell Ovidie of his plan, he calls her and she comes to him. The goat follows. They talk about Papa's plan to make the skis. Ovidie is excited! The goat gets extra hugs, and Papa gets questions. "When?" "When?" "When?"

13

Early Pictures of the farm in Elverum, Norway

The old farm house

The cow shed

The barn

The 'Stabbur' where food was stored

MORNING
Den Nye Dagen

It is dark, but it is morning!
   The cow moo-oo-oo's,
      the goat naa-aa's,
         the sheep baa-aa-aa,
            the horse neigh's,
               the chickens cluck,
                  while the rooster crows.

Once the animals are awake no one sleeps.
   Everyone is up and busy!
      Mama has milked the cow; the cow is Mama's.
      She has set the bread,
         made 'pannekaker' for breakfast,
            and is laying out the plans for the day. . .
         for the week.
            It is Monday.

Papa has tended the animals.
   The animals are given good care.
      Everyone in the family loves the animals.

The animals and the chickens are kept for what they
can provide for the family:
   the horses for hauling,
      the cow for milk,
         the goat also for milk for the favorite
         gjetost (goat's milk cheese),
            the sheep for wool to knit and weave,
            the chickens for eggs.

The animals and chickens are good providers;
   they are healthy,
      well-tended
      and safe.
In the winter the animals live warm and comfortable
in a large wooden shed at Hagenland.

Bows and Collars and Sunday Clothes

As daylight slowly comes the oil lamps are
put out one by one.
  Ovidie cleans the chimneys.
    The oil lamps will be ready with clean
    chimneys when evening comes.
      Cleaning the chimneys for the oil lamps
      is Ovidie's daily chore.

After cleaning each lamp Ovidie pauses to
adjust the large bow in her hair.
    Brother Aksel has brought Ovidie hair ribbons
    from Christiania, where he now lives.

Mama watches Ovidie fix the bow in her hair.
  She smiles.
    Aksel has been home for the weekend.
      It is good to see him 'all grown up'.
       Aksel 'var sa fin!'

Ovidie finishes cleaning the lamp on the
table and removes the chimney from the
lamp on the window ledge. She is still
thinking about church yesterday.

She had worn the blue bow in her hair and it had
made a hit. Everyone had noticed it. Now it is
Monday and a school day. She will wear it again.
Mama says that she should save it for Sundays.
Ovidie frowns and fastens the bow more tightly in
her hair.

"Why does everything have to be saved for Sunday?"
Ovidie thinks to herself. There is no use saying anything more to Mama.
     Ovidie has a Sunday dress. It is exactly like her
school dress, but it is newer. The Sunday dress still has
the two rows of tucks in it just above the hem. The tucks
will be let down when she is taller. When the tucks
are let down the dress will be her school dress.

Ovidie likes her Sunday dress.
Mama wove the cloth and made it
as she always has. But Ovidie
talked Mama into making a dark
blue collar for the Sunday dress.
Mama made the velvet collar from a pillow cover that
had worn in places. Ovidie is ever so pleased with
the addition of the collar to her dress. She likes
having a Sunday dress.
          But "Mama can say what she wants about saving
          everything for Sunday." Ovidie is thinking to
          herself. "Today I am wearing the bow in my
          hair to school and that is that!"

Ovidie continues with cleaning the chimneys for the oil lamps.

Mama's Mission

Mama is a midwife. At dawn this morning a
neighbor from far up on the hill sent her son
to ask Mama to come right away.

      Mama is fortunate today. The boy has come on
      horseback. Mama will ride back on the horse
      with him.
Most often Mama walks the long distances
up and down the hills , through snow and bad
weather to help deliver babies for folk all
around the area who need her help.

      It is cold and windy today.

          But, Mama is prepared for the ride on horseback
          and the long walk back.

               She has borrowed a pair of Papa's old
               trousers and is all bundled up under her skirts.

                    "People can think what they want,"
                    about 'my trousers'
                    she is saying. "I am the one who
                    has to go out in the snow and the cold
                    and ride on the back of a horse
                    to help deliver this baby".

Mama is known now for her ability to help.
She never trained to do the things she does.

          She has learned the knack of delivering babies
          and giving other aid just by doing it.
Last week a lumberjack from the sawmill had
come to Hagenland asking Mama to fix up the
arm he had injured on the job.

          Mama is always ready, quick and able to do
          what needs to done for someone.

Only known photograph of Ovidie's father,
Aksel Hagen

PAPA'S WORK

In church yesterday a villager had asked Papa
about a coffin needed for her deceased aunt who
had passed away the day before.
  Papa makes coffins.
        Papa had a coffin started.
                He will finish and deliver it today.

Tomorrow Papa will repair the door on a neighbor's
barn. The neighbor lives on the other side of the
river. The river is frozen. Papa can go right on
across it with his horse and wagon.

On the way home tomorrow Papa will stop on the
river to fish.
He will cut a chop a hole in the ice with his ax
  and drop his fishing line down the hole.
        Mama will have her freshly baked bread
                ready, and will cook the fish when Papa
                        arrives home.

DRESSMAKER

This morning Mama had watched Ovidie dress for Church.

As they sit quietly now waiting for Papa to arrive with the wagon, Mama is telling Ovidie that she has been thinking to have a Dressmaker come to the home to sew for them.

The girls are older now and it is better, she says, that a Dressmaker sew for them. She tells Ovidie that she will be able to work along with the Dressmaker to design her dresses, and in this way she will also be able to learn to sew for herself.

Mama will still weave some of the cloth and knit the underpinnings, stockings, mittens, gloves, hats, scarves and shawls.

The boys are gone now, but Papa likes the things she makes, so she will continue to sew for him.

The Dressmaker will live with them for whatever time it takes and will sew in exchange for room and board.

Ovidie is overjoyed with Mama's idea to have a Dressmaker come to the home to sew dresses for them.

She says that she will want skirts and blouses, too!

SECRET SHARED

On Sunday afternoon Mama has decided it is time
to visit her long time friend 'Aunt Olga'
who lives on the other side of the mountain.
  Papa will stay home to 'tend to things'.
    It had snowed a bit during the night,
    so this morning Papa had taken everyone to church
    in the wagon.
      But now Mama and Ovidie
      will ski walk to Aunt Olga's
      "It will be a beautiful walk in the snow", says Mama.

Mama will take Aunt Olga a pair of
ankle-to-knee leg warmers that she has just made for her.

    Everyone is saying how clever Mama is to
    create and design colorful leg warmers knitted,
    for the most part, from yarns left over from the
    shawls, sweaters, skirts, and underpinnings
    she regularly knits for the family.

      Knitting is Mama's hobby.
      She knits long into the nights,
      and it is her joy now to make these
      very practical and pretty leg warmers
      for special friends.

        "Good way to use up my left over yarns,"
        she says with satisfaction.

Aunt Olga was indeed glad to see her friends!
Said that she thought they "just might come",
helped them inside and made them comfortable
by the fire to warm up.

She brought out freshly made coffee and
a plate of small cakes, breads and cheeses.
Soon they were talking as they ate, talking and laughing,
especially laughing as they enjoyed
Aunt Olga's trying on the leg warmers.

Ovidie enjoys visiting Aunt Olga.
They find ways to have fun together.
The one thing Ovidie looks forward to is

when Aunt Olga takes her quietly aside
and makes her little gjetost and butter snacks-----
a layer of gjetost, a layer of butter,
a layer of gjetost, a layer of butter, and so on-----!

Mama does not approve of this extravagance.
Mama sys that Aunt Olga over-indulges Ovidie
with these treats, but she does not interfere
and so, the 'extravagance' continues.

Today while Mama is enjoying cake and coffee,
 she watches Aunt Olga and Ovidie across the room
giggling.

Mama smiles. She knows that it is
'gjetost-layered with-butter snacks time',
and she is happy that they are having
good fun together.

But, what Mama does NOT know is that
Ovidie has a secret, and that she
has just shared that secret
with Aunt Olga!

"Someday" says Ovidie,
"I will have all the gjetost and
butter snacks I can eat!"

More giggleling, more laughing!
It was a good visit!

Shoemakers Shoes

Mama is planning.

After school today, she wants Ovidie to do four more 'fingers' of knitting on the stocking she is making. One stocking is finished.

Mama wants the stockings completed so that they can be worn when the Shoemaker comes next week. The Shoemaker will stay with the family for several weeks. He will make shoes for everyone while he is there.

He will bring his lathe and hammer, sit by a fire in the back shed and shape the leather to fit each one's feet.

Ovidie is pouting. The thought of the Shoemaker coming has changed her mood! Mama knows that Ovidie does not want the Shoemaker's shoes. She wants shoes from the store.

Mama is distressed. Where does Ovidie get these ideas? None of her other children ever complained about the Shoemaker's shoes, the dresses, suits she makes and the hats she fixes over. The children have always been warm and comfortable. Not one of them has ever been 'without'.

She is thinking about last summer when she and Papa sheared the sheep. Mama had worked hard and long to clean and spin the wool, so that all could have new knitted

sweaters, stockings, caps, scarves, shawls
and mittens for the long, cold winter. The
girls even had new petticoats.

This year Mama had been able to lengthen
the dresses and trousers for another year's
wear. She knows how to make clothing a
bit larger so that they will last longer.

Mama will remember to instruct the Dressmaker,
when she comes to the home to sew, that
making dresses 'blousey' with substantial
tucks above the hems is important when
sewing for the growing Ovidie!

Ovidie is excited that a Dressmaker will come
to the home to sew, but the Shoemaker
coming-----UFF DA!!

Papa is sitting with his coffee. He knows why
Ovidie is sulking, and he knows what
Mama is thinking.

He tells Ovidie to finish the stocking and be
ready for the Shoemaker.

When she is confirmed in the Lutheran Church
will be time enough to buy ready-made shoes.

Papa says that then he will make her
new skis to fit the 'store' shoes.

Ovidie is pleased with this promise. She will
remind him of this promise from time to time.

Ovidie is already a good knitter. Mama knows
that Ovidie will finish her work after school
even though she herself will not be there.

SCHOOL

Ovidie is back from school now.
 She has kicked off her shoes, partly in
 disgust at the thought of having to endure
 another pair of the shoemaker's shoes.
 But, also, she must dry her stockings
 and rest her feet from having walked
 the long distance home from school.

Elverum School
Where Ovidie attended school

It is warm by the fire.
 Ovidie and Marianne have been eating bread
 and gjetost.
  Ovidie is telling Marianne about school.
   They are giggling.
    Ovidie is pleased that the teacher and
    other boys and girls at the school
    remarked about her bow.
     Arne and Lars kidded her about it.
     Lars tried to pull it off.
      She was pleased that it
      had been noticed!
       She will wear another
       bow tomorrow!

Pjuskin, Ovidie's favorite house cat, is curled
up in her knitting basket by the fire.
  Ovidie coaxes the big black and white cat out
  of the basket with a chunk of gjetost.
    Pjuskin loves gjetost.

Ovidie picks up her knitting.
  She will work carefully and steadily.
    Mama will be pleased to see that she has
    done more than the four-finger length she asked her to do.

Ovidie smiles. It is her secret that makes her
smile. Whenever she has been out and away from
home she comes back thinking about her secret.

BJARNE'S ACCORDIAN

About her secret. . . . . Ovidie is thinking that she must find a way
to dress like people do outside the village.

Bjarne had come to school today in a new suit.

It was not homemade!

Bjarne is leaving with his family for America in just two days.

His Papa had bought him the suit in a store in Christiania so that he
will look good for his trip to America.

Bjarne brought his accordian and played for the class. He really did 'look good',
thinks Ovidie, in his new clothes
as he played for the class.

Then it was sad to see Bjarne turn and give his
accordion to the teacher when he finished playing.
He explained that there was no room for the
accordion in the family's trunk.

He was leaving it with the teacher at the school so that someone
else could learn to play it.

Ovidie has decided that she will ask her brother,
Aksel, for a new dress and hat. . . . .
. . . . .from a store,
from Christiania.

Mama will not approve, but it is important to her secret!

Mama sews on Sunday

It is Sunday.

    Sunday's are very special.

        No one is permitted to work, except to tend
the animals.

            No one spins.

                No one weaves.

                    No one sews.

                        No one knits.

                            Spinning, weaving, sewing
and knitting are work.

Sunday is 'the Lord's Day'.

    The family has been to Elverum Kirke.

        They are at home now.

It is a warm spring afternoon.

    Mama is at the shed trying to figure out why
the door does not close tightly.

        "Can I help you?" says a small voice.
Mama turns and finds a young boy standing
there. Never in all her born days has Mama
seen a boy as dirty and ragged as the one
standing there.

        "Where do you come from?" Mama asks.
The boy explains that he has been staying
up at the sawmill for awhile. The men there
told him to come and see if Fru Hagen needed
someone to help her on the farm.

Mama is almost in tears. Behind the dirty face
and hair is a beautiful young boy. She will help
him.

"What's your name, son?" Mama asks.

    "Sverre", is the answer.

The reminder of the day is given over to Sverre.
He is cleaned up and fed.
Sunday, or not, Mama sews.
She cuts new knickers for Sverre from a
piece of her woven cloth and sews into the night.

She asssures excited Sverre that she has sewn
for her two sons. "They are grown now,"
she explains to Sverre "and have moved away
to the City. You stay with us. It will be good to
have you here to help."

Ovidie is shocked! Never has she seen Mama sew
on Sunday. She reminds Mama over and over that she
is sewing on Sunday.

Mama never stops sewing.
"This boy needs knickers and shirts," says Mama;
and then she explains that this is a different kind
of sewing, and says it in a tone that lets Ovidie
know that she intends to continue outfitting
Sverre, and that she is doing it with the Lord's
knowledge and blessing.

Sverre and Ovidie both attend Elverum School.

Sverre thoroughly enjoys school.

The teacher thoroughly enjoys Sverre.

She helps Sverre learn to play the accordian
left by Bjarne.

To everyone's surprise and joy
Sverre learns to play.

He plays and plays, sings and sings.

Up to the Hytte
To the little Sommer Høset
(Summer House)

It is summer.
 It is the day for moving on up to the Sommer Høset
in the mountains.
  Peder and Aksel have come home to Hagenland
  to help transport the family, the animals and
  all of the food and belongings needed for the
  stay at the Hytte.

Trudging up-up-up through the woods is Mama with
her cow,
  Aksel, Marianne, Ovidie and Sverre following
   with the sheep, the goat and carrying the
   chickens.

It is exciting. It is tiring.
 The cow moo-oo-o's,
  the sheep baa-aa-a,
   the chickens cluck,
    the children laugh and sing and play.
Mama swings along, picnic basket and possessions
loaded on the back of her cow.

The climb will take most of the day.
 The woods are thick.
  The hills are high.
   The climb is long.
Mama is used to climbing the hills.
 She knows the way.
  She leads them onward.

They move slowly upward with talk and thoughts
of summer at the Hytte- - - -
      the beauty there,
          the mountain tops,
             the fields for growing,
                streams to play in,
                   fish to catch,
                      berries to pick,
                         the long, long days.

Other families are there for the summer, too.
      There will be children to play with at the Hytte.

Papa has stayed behind with Peder 'to tend to
things' at Hagenland. Papa will come up to
the Hytte from time to time to haul and
help, but will not stay long. Papa always feels
that his place is at Hagenland to 'tend to things'.

Hurray! Mama has found a perfect spot for the
picnic lunch.
       Aksel is weary,
            the children are hungry,
                 the animals are thirsty.
Mama and Marianne seat the group on a woven throw
on the ground by a stream.
       Out come the gjetost sandwiches and assorted small cakes.
           Everyone eats.

             The animals drink from the stream.
And then!- - the discovery!
       Berries to be picked and eaten by the handful
       are everywhere.

The animals enjoy the berries, too.
       These are the berries they find each
       summer at the Hytte.
           It is a delicious treat, and a happy
           thought that the summer house must be
           close now.

              Soon the Hagen Family from the
              valley will be high up and happy
              in the mountains, renewing friendships
              and enjoying the beautiful outdoors.

              Mama is reminding everyone that
              there will be plenty of work to do there.
              "We will work hard," she says,
              "then there will be plenty for the winter."

SVERRE'S ACCORDIAN
Now

Sverre is 16 years old.

He has taken a cabin-boy job on board an
American bound ship.

Sverre will stay in America.

The teacher is sad to see Sverre leave Norway.

Sverre has no possessions to take along, and so----
she gives him the accordion that Bjarne had to
leave behind when he left for America.

Sverre thanks the teacher and the class.
He plays Norway's national hymn for them,
"Ja vi elsker dette landet"---
"Yes We Love this Land of Ours".

Everyone sings, the children laugh and clap,
the teacher 'tears'.

So, Sverre leaves Elverum, Norway,
accordion case in hand, looking good,
and happy with memories of life at
Hagenland.

* * * * * *

Sverre lived at Hagenland for almost two years.

Mama 'took in' other persons needing a home from
time to time.

Sverre was the youngest.

Sverre stayed the longest.

Old Postcard

Elverum Kirke/Elverum Church

Elverum Kirke from 1738. Richly carved and gilt
furniture from the 1700's. Medival crucifix

Photo taken 1934

CONFIRMATION

Ovidie is fourteen years old and is preparing to
be Confirmed in the Lutheran Church.
Ovidie will attend weekly classes at Elverum Kirke.

    It is six kilometers to Elverum Kirke. She will
    ski walk alone starting early in the morning
    while it is still dark. It will be dinnertime
    and dark when she arrives home.

       Ovidie is strong,
          healthy,
             active,
                anxious,
                   excited,
                      determined!
    She will have no trouble making the long
    walk to and from Elverum Kirke for the
    Confirmation classes.

Papa managed to get the money together so that
Ovidie could buy new shoes from a store in
Christiania.

    He has made Ovidie new skis to fit the 'store-bought'
    shoes.

       Ovidie is thrilled and happy with these new
       shoes and skis.

Mama can see that Ovidie is becoming quite a young lady.
    Mama has let the tucks down on Ovidie's favorite
    Sunday dress, and put a new small round collar on it.
    Ovidie will wear one of her ribbon bows at the
    neck of the dress.

       Mama is busy making Ovidie a complete set of
       underpinnings and stockings. She wants Ovidie
       to be warm, and completely outfitted for her
       Confirmation classes.

Ovidie's Confirmation Bible

Ovidie's Norwegian Bible
presented to her when she was confirmed
and read throughout most of her lifetime.
Leatherbound
with gold leaf inscriptions
(barely visable in this picture)
Bibelen (The Bible) toward the top
and on the lower edge her name
Ovidie Hagen

Photo taken in 1989 and shown with her large type
Norwegian Bible, a gift from daughters on her 80th birthday.

Ovidie is bright.
      She has a remarkable memory.
            She is capable,
                will study hard
                    and she will do good.
Through Confirmation Ovidie will
      increase in wisdom,
            and in stature,
                and in favor with God
                  and man.
The Lutheran Pastor, her teacher, her Mama and Papa,
everyone will look with pride and admiration on the
serious manner with which young Ovidie moves through
the Confirmation.

The little girl Christened when born,
      taught faithfully in the home and in the church
      through the years,
            instructed in the Confirmation classes,
                has now openly and officially confirmed her faith
                  for herself,
                    to her God,
                      to her church,
                        to her family.

Ja, alt skal bli bra med barna!

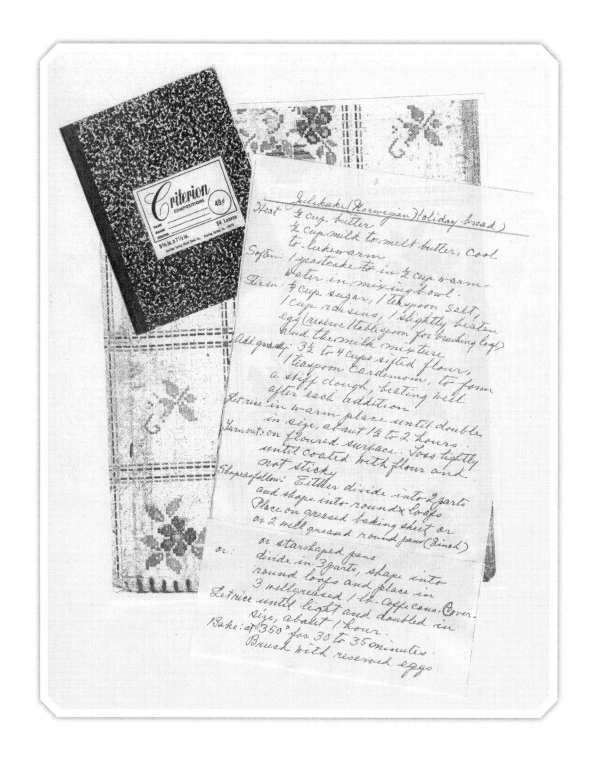

Recipe for Julekake
(Norwgian Holiday Bread)

From one of Mother's handwritten cookbooks. Virtually all of her cooking
and baking was from these carefully maintained hand written books. Baking
Julekake was a favorite family Christmas tradition.

Julekake
Traditional Christmas Bread

"Mama, we have baked enough Julekake for the
village!" laughs Ovidie.

Ovidie worked with Mama to make the Julekake
and cookies.

Ovidie has decided that baking and cooking
are her favorite things to do.

Mama told Ovidie today that she is a
good cook, and especially with breads.

"You have the knack", says Mama.

Mama wants her to go to cooking school.
"There is a cooking school in
Christiania", Mama said. "Some of the
girls who go there plan to go to
America." She went on to say that if
you can cook you can always find work
in America.

Ovidie could not believe what she was hearing.

She wanted to throw the dough right up on the
ceiling like she had done when she was a toddler.

Ovidie is excited about Mama's idea!

"But why is Mama saying this to me?"
she is asking to herself.

"Does Mama think I will go to America?"

"Does Mama know my secret?"

47

She has never felt this at peace with herself,
so internally happy and grateful.

CHRISTMAS

It is Christmas Eve.
Ovidie is resting on the bench by the fire holding
Pjuskin in her arms.
    She has never felt this at peace with herself,
        so internally happy and grateful.
            Her home and her life seem to have been
            touched with a bit of heaven.
                So pleased is she - - -!

The house has been made ready for Christmas- -
    cleaned from beams to floor,
        greens cut and placed over doors, windows,
        pictures and on the shelves,
            furniture pushed back as far to the walls
            as it will go,
                and in the center of the room is the
                large tree that Papa brought in
                yesterday.

                    The Christmas tree is trimmed with
                    nature forms handmade by the children
                    through the years.

Now Ovidie is watching Pjuskin sniff the packages
    under the Christmas tree.

        Mama reminds Pjuskin that there is nothing
        there for him. Ovidie tells the excited Pjuskin to
        wait for the lutefisk.

        She pulls a piece of yarn across the floor
        and up into the air. Pjuskin runs and leaps after it,
        then settles down at Ovidie's feet to wait for lutefisk.

Ovidie is looking at the packages.
Last Christmas there was an orange and some nuts
in her package. She will never forget the special joy of
receiving that orange for Christmas!

Papa is bringing Aksel and Peder and their young
wives up from Christiania. Papa has greens on the wagon
and bells on the horse's harness.

Soon there will be laughter and talking and singing
when everyone arrives.

Mama's lutefisk, rice pudding and julekake
will please all the hungry appetites.

The family will sing and dance- - - - -
holding hands, they will
sing and dance around the
Christmas tree in the middle of the room.

After Mama's supper,

after dancing around the Christmas tree,

after all have received gifts,

after everything begins to quiet down- - - -

no matter how much everyone has already sung, and

no matter how many times everyone has sung
Mama's favorite Christmas Eve carol,
she will request it one more time and all will sing it,
one more time, from grateful hearts- - - -

"Jeg Er Så Glad Hver Julekveld"--
"I am so glad each Christmas Eve."

When finally the festivities have ended, and all are asleep,
JULENISSEN is for sure expected to visit Hagenland.

JULENISSEN, a mischievous type troll with a toothy grin,
is believed to quietly, lest he be discovered, wander around
on Christmas Eve from home to home, barn to barn and
shed to shed in search of treats.

A part of the Hagen's Christmas Eve ritual before retiring is
Mama and Ovidie's trip to the barn
to leave flatbreads or cookies for the nisse.

They can all now rest assured that no harm
will come to Hagenland this night.
They have appeased Julenissen
and he will go elsewhere with his pranks.

Early in the morning on Christmas day the family will travel
over the miles of new fallen snow to Elverum Kirke for worship
in celebration of the Christchilld's birth,

     and to wish all friends from the beautifully
     lit-up and highly decorated friendly village a heartfelt 'God Jul',

          before retuning to Hagenland for Mama's
          Christmas Day dinner--her feast of the
          family's traditional favorites which have been
          for week's in the making!

The glow of memories of Hagenland's
family celebration of Christmas
will brighten Ovidie's life----well, forever!!!

Aksel's Plan

Everyone is at the front window peering down the roadway, taking turns, back and forth watching for Aksel's arrival.

Aksel is coming up from Christiania today for a visit and to have dinner with his family at Hagenland.

This is to be a very special visit. Aksel has a new friend. He is a school teacher in Christiania. He is handsome, hardworking and fun to be with, likes to go places and do things and, important to Aksel and Mama, is that the school teacher yearns to some day farm. Akesl has, with excitement, arranged this visit so that his school teacher friend can see the farm and meet Ovidie. Ovidie is smart--Aksel knows that she and the school teacher will 'hit it off.'

Aksel's Plan:

Ovidie and his school teacher friend will marry, he believes.

The newlyweds will farm and raise a family at Hagenland.

It will be a good life for Ovidie, for Mama and for Marianna, and most importantly, Hagenland, the centuries old family homestead will be retained and maintained in good order!

This is an especially happy day full of promise for everyone, well, for everyone except Ovidie who only knows about the ' meet the school teacher' part.

* * * * * * *

The 'back and forth' to the window continues. Mama is thinking how clean the freshly washed windows look, and as she glances proudly and anxiously around the room, is pleased that all is in order. *"Ja, she thinks, the girls have done a fine job!* "Alt er ferdi!*" All is ready.

And then, she calls to Ovidie, a bit hesitant, straining to see if what she sees from the window is-----yes indeed----"Ovidie", she calls again with excitement "put the coffeepot on, the wagon is coming. I can see the horse, yes they are coming now. Ja, godt, ja, ja godt!"

Ovidie, with Marianna there, too, takes a quick look. The horse drawn wagon that Aksel has borrowed for today's special visit has come into view. Ovidie mutters "Uff-da" fixes her hair, secures the large bow she is wearing and goes off to make the coffee.

Marianna giggles and follows along.

Soon the aroma of coffee blends in with that left earlier by Mama's preparation of everyone's favorite 'fiskeboller', fishballs for the meal she has planned.

* * * * * *

The horse drawn wagon arrives.

Aksel and the school teacher are in their "Sunday best'.

Everyone is overjoyed as they greet
each other warmly, and
move on inside for coffee
and Mama's fiskeboller meal.

* * * * * * *

It WAS a good day for all, including Ovidie!
Ovidie liked the teacher.

She was flattered by his attention to her, and

"yes", she would accept his invitation
to go to Christiania the next week
to meet him there.

In fact, Ovidie went to Christiania many times in the months that followed
to spend good times with the school teacher.
Aksel was with them, too.

Ovidie enjoyed the 'good times'.
She enjoyed the city, Christiania, Norway's capital city.
She enjoyed going places and doing new things.
She had now acquired the new 'store-bought' dresses,
hats and shoes that she had always wanted!

* * * * * * *

But, marriage to the school teacher was not to be.

To everyone's heartbreak Ovidie called off
the friendship with no explanation.

It was not, never had been, Ovidie's plan to stay at Hagenland and live on in
Norway!

She could not be persuaded otherwise.

The seed of her secret dream, so deeply implanted
since childhood, had over the years
sprouted, taken root and at this point was
with vigor continuing to grow and seemed,
in fact, about ready to burst into bloom!

If anything, her trips to the big city of Christiania
with the 'going places' and 'doing things'
gave nurture to her dream of a different lifestyle
in a place other than Hagenland.

But, though it was becoming evident to those close to her
that she might be ' up to something' and
at times seemed even to be happily smug,
Ovidie never did share with those closest to her
the excitement stirring within herself-----her hope,
her longings, her dreams and in fact, her plans for-----
well, that continued to be her secret.

Nor could Aksel and his school teacher friend,
nor even Mama, all so fraught with hurt
and disappointment, talk openly
either with Ovidie, or about Ovidie's complete
rejection of what had seemed
so perfect a plan.

They could only just sit quietly
amongst themselves,
shake their heads in disbelief and
occasionally confirm for each other
that strong-willed Ovidie, though adored,
did certainly have a mind of her own,
always had;

and then, more quietly whisper, that she'd
probably someday,
again to the heartbreak of all,
do something way out crazy,
like leave her
beloved Hagenland
with its potential for a good life,
to immigrate to America with all of its 'unknowns'.

More head shaking.

CHANGES

Mama's health is failing--she is sixty years old.
It has been three years since she laid Papa to rest.

      He is in the church yard at Elverum Kirke.

          Mama has planted red geraniums and blue
          lobelia at the grave site, and tends the
          flowers after services on Sunday.

             She seems alone.

Ovidie is seventeen years old. She stays by her
Mama's side.

      Ovidie is attractive

         stylish,

            hardworking,

               and never alone.

Ovidie has a close friend Càmela.

      Ovidie and Camela are often seen in the village
      shopping together.

         Ovidie and Camela share a secret!

Mama and the girls are doing all they can to
keep things going at Hagenland.

      Ovidie cooks and bakes most of the time.

         Mama 'tends to things' as Papa used to do.

         Marianne works hard, too.

The work is endless.

      Mama, tireless in the past, must now take
      'her rest'.

         Mama has a large growth on the side of her
         head. Summer and winter she wears a
         headscarf so as to cover the growth.

Mama's Cow

One morning Mama just could
not get out of bed.
    This was serious.
        Who would milk Mama's Cow?
            The cow would not let anyone else milk her.
Mama and Ovidie solved the problem.
    Ovidie dressed in Mama's clothes--even wore
the shawl around her head.
        She went silently into the shed and was able
to milk the cow.
            When finished, Ovidie patted the cow on
the back and told her 'takk.' She was a
good cow afterall.
                With this, the cow knew that she had been
fooled. She gave Ovidie a good hard
thrashing with her tail.
                    It hurt, but it was worth it to
have the milk- -
                        and to see how Mama laughed and
laughed when told how her cow had
turned to see, that indeed, she had
been 'tricked' and reacted with the tail
thrashing.

Only Known
Pictures of Ovidie's Mama,
Hanna Hagen

ᴍᴀᴍᴀ ɪs ʀᴇᴀᴅʏ

Mama is resting in her favorite chair by the window. The chair is where she always sits to knit.

 She had closed her eyes for awhile with the knitting on her lap. Now she has opened her eyes
  and is ready to start again.

Mama is knitting a new light colored headscarf from homespun wool that she 'has on hand'.

 When finished, the scarf will be carefully folded and placed with other new and 'fixed up' things in a chest.

 The chest is actually one of Papa's burial boxes that was about finished when he passed.

Mama has told Ovidie that she wants to have a complete outfit for herself fixed and ready in Papa's box.

 "Always good to have a few things laid away for when you need them", says Mama.

Mama has always been ready;
 ready for each new day,
  for each new week,
   for breakfast, for 'middag,' for supper,

ready for visits,
 ready with clothes,
  ready to trudge the hills
   to help deliver a baby,

ready to take someone into the home,
 to pack the family, animals and food
  up to the 'hytte' in the warm months,

yes, ready for summer,
 ready for winter,
  ready for Christmas!

The knitting again drops to her lap. Mama's scarf is finished. She admires it with satisfaction as she folds it, and then while smoothing out the wrinkles looks around and calls for Ovidie.

Grave Site

Elverum Kirke
Pictures taken 1951

Hanna
Matheasdatter
Bjølsethagen
Born December 6, 1846
Died July 24, 1907

Aksel Pedersen
Bjølsethagen
Born November 20, 1840
Died November 26, 1904

"Ovidie, in that last box that Papa made out there in the shed", she
instructs "open the lid and put this scarf with the
other things you'll see there." Ovidie grabs her wool cape
and skips off with Mama's scarf.
She knows about the 'box' and the 'fixed up things',
but never questions. Things like the 'box' and its
contents are just never talked about.

Mama puts her head back to rest against the cushioned chair.
Thin-lipped, but with a glimmer of smile,
she sighs. She has picked up her well-worn Bible from
the lamp table.

Mama is at peace.

Mama is ready.

Mama Hanna died of pneumonia that same year.

She was laid to rest beside Papa in the

church yard at Elverum Kirke.

First Photo in America

In Chicago area,
having traveled by Immigrant Train
to the Midwest from Boston Harbor

Leaving Home

Ovidie is alone at Hagenland with Marianne in her care.

It is not possible for the girls to maintain the farm.

The homestead is auctioned---the money divided
among the children.

It is no longer a secret what Ovidie will do.

She will use her inheritance to book passage
to America!

Her friend, Camela, will go, too.

And so, at age eighteen, Ovidie Hagen leaves
her beloved home and homeland
to set sail for America.

The secret dream she has carried since childhood
is now to become reality!

The young lady who has learned to work hard,

steadily and carefully,

who has learned to be resourceful and
to save money,

who has been confirmed in the Lutheran Church,
and knows to read the Bible and pray,

this intrepid young lady enters America through
Boston Harbor in 1907-----

stylish,

vivacious,

courageous,

and--using her new name, VIDA!

Bringing with her to America from her childhood in
Norway are the memories, and a legacy of faith based life lessons- - - - -
"packaged into the very soul of her being- - - -".

As she enters Boston Harbor, Vida swings proudly along

with her new suitcase in hand. Nothing 'homemade' has been

packed. She has outfitted herself with 'store purchased'

attire just right, she thinks, for coming to America.

    Vida is visably feeling prepared and ready to start her new

    life in this land of promise!

Not visable, and perhaps not even realized by Vida,

is the beautifully wrapped gift of faith based life lessons,

    her legacy from her Mama Hanna,

        packaged into the very soul of her being,

           not new or 'purchased', but rather,

                carefully instilled,

                    not preached, but lived,

                        through all of the years

                            of her growing up in Norway.

Was life here in America to be, in fact, the adventure she

had expected?

Were the values instilled at Hagenland sufficient for Vida

when she faced the diversity of challenges in her new life?

Did how mother Vida pull from those internalized

faith based values to live her life fully to age 101 years

leave a "Legacy of Life Lessons" for her children?

Is that Legacy worthy of an attempt to write about it

so that others might reflect on the merits of her life,

and thusly, find inspiration?

Would Mama Hanna and Mother Vida be the most

amazed to know that as simple folk they had so

'inspired'?

Answers: Yes, yes, yes, yes, and you bet!

AFTERWARD

Married

AFTERWARD

Subsequent to Ovidie's arrival in America through Boston
Harbor using her new name Vida, she would

- locate in the Chicago area earning a living as a cook for private families

- while learning to speak and write English,

- eventually relocate to the Philadelphia area, and

- marry Eugene Engh the handsome young seaman and 'good dancer' she had actually met, and enjoyed being with, on board the ship to America,

- find marriage to her seaman to be fraught with long separations,

- and the stress of financial hardship, especially through the Great Depression of the 1930's when seamen working as stewards on board the yachts of the well-to-do were hard put to find regular work,

- be widowed in 1944 when the Mississippi River claimed the life of husband, Eugene.

RIVER VICTIM IDENTIFIED
A body found in the Mississippi Monday near Venice in Plaquemines Parish today was identified as that of Eugene Engh, 55, a cook on a Coyle coal tug. Death, according to Coroner B. R. Slater, was assigned to natural causes.

Husband, Eugene, enjoying the fine up-scale life style
of the well-to-do owners of the yachts on which he worked.

At time of his death he had been a long time member of
Sons of Norway Lodge
and was a
33rd Degree Mason

He spent time with wife and family
when yachts docked in Philadelphia.

- be naturalized as an American citizen in 1946,

- have her name Vida officially court approved as a part of the naturalization process,

- keep busy and involved with family and the home, steadfastly attending to

  her faith,

    her church,

      food,

        clothing,

          cleaning,

            sewing,

              knitting,

- survive illnesses, many serious--physical, emotional, disabling-- with courage and good spirit,

- find that cooking could help her to 'find work in America' as her Mama Hanna had said, taught and encouraged!

CITIZENSHIP

- be enthusiastic about her American citizenship with its voting and other privileges, yet never loosing her love of Norway.

DAUGHTERS

Ruth

Dorothy

Betty

Our glance backward has revealed,

and underscored,

the courage and resourcefulness

of our mother--traits instilled while

growing up in Norway.

Through both good and lean years,

    Mother,

        Vida Engh,

            Ovidie Hagen

has by her example passed on to

her three daughters

    Ruth Myrtle

        Dorothy Marguerite

            Betty Florence

strengths and a basic value system

for which we are grateful.

    Thank you,

        Mother

1950 Photograph taken while on a family visit

Top left: Ruth Engh Erb (Married to Arthur Kenneth Erb)
Top right: Dorothy Engh Gift (Married to Joseph Luther Gift)
Bottom with our mother: Betty Engh
(Single-later married to Bjarne Eugen Pettersen)

MOTHER

Lovingly remembered

Takk for alt!

And, A Final Word From Scripture—

Be Very Careful Never To Forget What You Have Seen God Doing For You. May His Miracles Have A Deep And Permanent Effect Upon Your Lives! Tell Your Children And Your Grandchildren About The Glorious Miracles He Did. —So That They Will Learn Always To Reverence Me, And So That They Can Teach My Laws To Their Children.

Deuteronomy 4:9, 10 Living Bible Paraphrased